laura james
the new **AGA** cook

laura james
the new **AGA** cook

absolute press

First published as three separate titles in
The New Aga Cook series in 2003:
Breakfast and Brunch
Good Food Fast
Cooking for Kids

This collated edition first published
in Great Britain in 2007
by **Absolute Press**
Scarborough House
29 James Street West
Bath BA1 2BT
Phone 44 (0) 1225 316013
Fax 44 (0) 1225 445836
E-mail info@absolutepress.co.uk
Website www.absolutepress.co.uk

Publisher
Jon Croft
Commissioning Editor
Meg Avent
Design
Tim James and Matt Inwood
Photography
Andy Davies
Food Stylist
Penny Chambers

ISBN 9781904573784

Printed and bound by Printer Trento, Italy

contents

introduction

I learned to cook on an Aga and, to this day, have never quite managed to master a conventional cooker with quite the same aplomb. The Aga, quite simply, makes cooking easier. It's forgiving, gentle and really does make everything taste better.

I love to cook and feel about a full fridge, stuffed with possibilities, the way other women feel about Christian Louboutin shoes or Alice Temperley dresses. And, as one of the great thrills in life is cooking for the people one loves, I was thrilled to spend enforced time in the kitchen testing recipes and coercing my friends and family to rate each dish.

I'm not a chef or home economist, simply
a busy working mother who loves to cook
and enjoys a kitchen full of people. And
it's in this spirit that this book is offered.

Laura James
Norfolk, 2007

breakfast and brunch

a word about breakfast and brunch

When, recently married and impossibly young, my husband and I rented a sweet little cottage with an Aga, I fell in love with it at first sight, although I can now admit to having been slightly daunted by the thought of cooking on it.

We moved in on a Saturday and on the Sunday morning I got up and cooked a huge brunch for all the friends who'd helped us. It tasted amazing and my husband joked that I must have been taking secret cookery classes. In fact, it was simply the Aga's ability to compensate for the shortcomings of youth.

Since then, Sunday morning Aga breakfasts and brunches have become a ritual for us. For me, there are few things as enjoyable as spending time around a crowded kitchen table eating delicious food with people I adore.

I remember being told over and again as a child that breakfast was the most important meal of the day.

But as I was growing up (and certainly during my teenage years) a cup of coffee and anything snatched from the pantry before I flew out the door seemed to be the order of the day.

Now I have children of my own it's really lovely to sit down for a proper family breakfast and to chat about everything that's going on.

Of course breakfast can be whatever you want it to be. But there's something elemental about starting the day with food you've prepared yourself, rather than something out of a box.

In this section I've included recipes – many of them deliberately loose and informal – for some of my favourites.

egg, bacon and sausage muffins

I hate with a passion those red and yellow fast-food outlets you see in every town. But most children don't and I have to admit that, while I don't enjoy the mass-produced version of this dish, if it's made with the very best ingredients it's really fantastic.

1 egg
1 sausage
1 rasher of bacon
Half a tomato
1 English muffin

Line a roasting tin with Bake-O-Glide and place the sausages on the rack. Cook in the roasting oven on the first set of runners for about 10 minutes.

Take the tin out, turn the sausages and slide in the tomatoes underneath the rack. Cook for a further 5 minutes.

Add the bacon and cook for about 7 minutes, turning once. While this is going on, lightly grease a round piece of Bake-O-Glide and place it on the simmering plate. Break the egg on to the Bake-O-Glide and close the lid. The egg will only take a couple of minutes, so keep checking to ensure it's done just how you like it.

While the egg is cooking, toast the muffin in the Aga toaster on the boiling plate and remove the sausages, bacon and tomatoes from the roasting oven. Butter the muffin lightly. Cut the sausage in half lengthways and place on the bottom of the muffin. Put the bacon on top, then the fried egg and, finally, the tomato. Then simply sit back and enjoy…

Makes one muffin

Enjoy a full breakfast in one truly delicious hit....

chill-out pancakes

Weekends were made for children. And pancakes were made for weekends. I love making up the batter with the children and enjoying their faces as they await the first to come out of the pan…

A little butter
8 rashers of streaky bacon
115g (4 oz) of plain flour
1 teaspoon of baking powder
Pinch of salt
3 eggs, beaten
140ml (5 fl oz) of full-fat milk
Maple syrup

Fry the bacon and set aside. Sift all the dry ingredients into a large bowl and make a well. Then gradually add the eggs, slowly adding the milk as you go, until the batter is smooth. Or, if time is tight, simply blitz all the ingredients in a blender.

You can cook the pancakes directly on the simmering plate or on a round piece of Bake-O-Glide on the simmering plate, having simply smeared either with a little butter. Place single tablespoons of batter on to the surface, allowing them room to spread. Once the pancakes puff up and start to bubble, turn them over and cook for a further minute or two.

Then simply place the pancakes in little piles on plates and criss-cross each one with the bacon.

Pour over the maple syrup and enjoy!

Serves 4

Try these pancakes with bananas, blueberries, strawberries…

eggy bread

This was the first dish my eldest daughter attempted. I remember her frown of concentration and the look of triumph as she watched us all tucking in enthusiastically!

1 large egg
Splash of full-fat milk
2 slices of bread, preferably thick and
   slightly stale
Butter, for frying

It's hopelessly twee, I know, but my children adore Eggy Bread when it's cut into cute shapes, such as rabbits, ducks or stars.

Biscuit cutters are perfect for this job and the only limit to the shapes possible is your imagination – or, more probably, your embarrassment threshold.

Beat the egg with the milk. Soak the bread into the mixture for about a minute.
Melt the butter in a frying pan on the boiling plate then move to the simmering plate.

Place the egg-soaked bread in the frying pan and fry for a couple of minutes before turning over to fry the other side for a few more.

Serves 1

...or simply just a sprinkling of sugar.

the perfect bacon sandwich

Ad campaigns have been built around it. Poems have been penned in its honour. There are awards in its name. Much is made of the ultimate bacon sandwich – here's my version.

Knob of butter
3 rashers of good-quality bacon
2 slices of thick white bread

Because the Aga is always on, it's perfect for a quick bacon sandwich. I often use my kitchen like a takeaway and whip up a quick bacon sandwich to eat in the car. Rather than using the pan juices, my husband prefers his bacon sandwich to drip with butter and be made with the thickest, freshest brown bread.

Key to getting it right is buying the very best bacon. My favourite is from Duchy Originals – the fat seems to crisp up in a way no other bacon does. Simply divine.

In a pan on the simmering plate, fry the bacon in the butter until the fat has started to turn slightly golden. Take it out of the frying pan and dip one side of the bread into the pan.

Make up the sandwich and devour. You could, of course, add ketchup or brown sauce, but personally I regard this as sacrilege.

Makes 1 sandwich

Wash it down with a huge mug of builders' tea!

devilled kidneys

Once a favoured breakfast dish, Devilled Kidneys fell out of fashion for a while. Now, they're very much back in vogue and are simply perfect for cold winter mornings.

8 lambs' kidneys
25g (1 oz) of butter
2 teaspoons of Worcestershire sauce
1 tablespoon of tomato purée
1 tablespoon of lemon juice
1 tablespoon of French mustard
Pinch of cayenne pepper
Salt and freshly ground black pepper
1 tablespoon of chopped parsley

Remove the skin from the kidneys, cut them in half and cut away the cores. Heat the butter in a frying pan on the simmering plate and cook the kidneys for about three minutes on each side.

To make the sauce, mix together all the remaining ingredients, except the parsley. In the pan, pour the devil sauce over the kidneys and stir so that they are evenly coated. Sprinkle with the chopped parsley and serve with toast.

Grilled tomatoes make a fabulous accompaniment. Slice eight tomatoes, sprinkle with sea salt and freshly ground black pepper and grill at the top of the roasting oven for about 15 minutes.

Serves 4

This devilishly good sauce has many uses.

baked eggs

This recipe takes a moment to put together and doesn't need any attention while it's cooking. So you can go off and have a shower or walk the dog. Whatever makes you smile....

A little butter
1 slice of Parma ham
1 egg
1 tablespoon of single cream
25g (1 oz) of grated Red Leicester
   or Cheddar cheese
Salt and pepper

As these are cooked in individual dishes, I've listed the ingredients for one. Obviously you can make as many as you like and the method doesn't change.

Serves 1

Grease a ramekin dish with butter. Put the ham in the base of the dish. Break an egg into it and spoon over the cream. Top with the grated cheese, salt and pepper.

Stand the dish on a baking tray on the grid shelf on the floor of the roasting oven and cook for 15–20 minutes until the whites of the eggs are firm.

These are delicious with a warmed granary roll.

breakfast kebabs

This recipe is one of my friend Patty's favourites. It's a fabulous way to encourage children to eat a proper breakfast as they tend to be wildly excited by its novelty value.

6 wooden skewers
6 rashers of streaky bacon
3 sausages
24 cherry tomatoes
Olive oil (not extra virgin)
Salt and pepper

Soak the skewers in water for about five minutes; this will stop them burning in the oven and they'll stay that lovely blonde colour.

Cut each bacon rasher in half and roll up tight. Crudely slice the sausages and thread them on to the skewers with the bacon and tomatoes. Brush with a little oil and sprinkle with salt and pepper.

Cook in a roasting tin on the top set of runners of the roasting oven for about 30 minutes, turning halfway through. Serve with hot buttered toast and scrambled eggs (see page 28).

Serves 6

If you like mushrooms, add a few to the skewers.
The joy is that you can make them up as you wish.

best-ever scrambled eggs

There's something about good scrambled eggs that makes them suitable for all weathers and all moods.

6 large organic eggs
50ml (2 fl oz) of double cream
2 tablespoons of chopped smoked
　salmon
Black pepper

I'm sure wars have started over the perfect texture for scrambled eggs. I like mine to be slightly wet and a little runny, whereas my daughter likes them to be much more formed and almost omelette-like in their texture.

Whatever your preference, it's important to use the best possible ingredients. At last count we had two dozen chickens, who seem to be prolific egg producers.

But these days the supermarkets, too, offer a decent range of eggs. It's a matter of buying well. The real secret to perfect scrambled eggs is to make sure you use the right pan. Aga Shops sell an excellent Aga non-stick cast-aluminium pan which should ensure perfect results every time. Beat together the eggs and cream. Add the black pepper and smoked salmon and pour into the pan.

Place the pan on the simmering plate for about five minutes, stirring occasionally, until you have perfectly fluffy scrambled eggs. Serve immediately.

Serves 4

We just adore these given a kick with grated cheese and chives instead of the salmon.

aga kippers

Kippers are delicious, but the smell can hang around for days. However, if you cook them in the Aga roasting oven this shouldn't be a problem and they're perfect for icy winter mornings.

1 kipper
Knob of butter

I was always slightly wary of kippers – don't ask me why, perhaps I was frightened by one as a child! I also, quite wrongly, imagined them being difficult to get right, when in fact they are the easiest things in the world to cook. My aversion turned to true love one cold morning at the Balmoral Hotel in Edinburgh. A very smart lady sitting on the next table polished off a plate in record time and then promptly ordered another.

In a *When Harry Met Sally* moment, I demanded 'what she's having' and haven't looked back since.

As soon as the first leaf falls off the first tree I'm at the fishmonger's ordering a trawler-load of kippers. There's something about eating them in cold weather that makes one feel truly cosseted. I also confess to eating them for lunch, supper and, on a particularly hard day, afternoon tea as well. How many kippers you cook is, of course, up to you. The method remains the same.

Simply add a knob of butter to each kipper, wrap in foil and place in a roasting tin. Cook on the third set of runners in the roasting oven for 15–20 minutes.

Serves 1

The Aga seems ideally suited to doing kippers. The stored heat gives perfect results every time.

aga porridge

There's something rather romantic about making up porridge late on a Saturday night, putting it in the simmering oven and coming down to it all creamy and delicious on a grey Sunday morning.

600ml (20 fl oz) of water
75g (2³/₄ oz) of pinhead oatmeal
   (Hamlyns is fabulous)
Sugar to taste
Couple of tablespoons of double cream

For me, this dish will always taste of Christmas as it's the one thing I can persuade my children to eat before they start on the present opening.

Last thing at night, bring the water to the boil in a heavy-based pan and stir in the oatmeal. Bring back to the boil and then move the pan to the simmering plate for a couple of minutes. Cover the pan with a tightly fitting lid and move to the grid shelf on the floor of the simmering oven (or the warming oven in a four-oven Aga). Leave overnight. In the morning, stir well and add sugar and cream.

Of course, if you'd prefer a more authentic taste, you should forget about the sugar and cream and simply add salt.

Serves 2

blueberry muffins

These are muffins to die for. I often put them in the children's lunchboxes or have them with a mug of hot chocolate at bedtime. When I'm busy I serve them warm with ice cream as a pudding.

200g (8 oz) of plain flour
125g (4^1/$_2$ oz) of caster sugar
2 teaspoons of baking powder
Pinch of salt
1 egg
150ml (5 fl oz) of full-fat milk
100g butter
125g (3^3/$_4$ oz) of blueberries

In my mind at least these muffins are the staple basics of every American breakfast. When I cook them I feel like a '50s housewife waiting for her husband to leap over the picket fence with the Sunday papers, followed by a dog called Skip.

Mix the dry ingredients together, then beat in the egg, milk and butter. Gently fold in the blueberries. Put the muffin cases into a muffin tray and spoon in the mixture.

With the grid shelf on the floor of the roasting oven, put in the muffin tray and cook for 25–30 minutes.

If the muffins start to brown too quickly, slide in the cold plain shelf on the third set of runners.

In a four oven Aga, place the muffin tray on the grid shelf on the third set of runners of the baking oven. Cook for about 25 minutes.

Makes about 12

strawberry and white chocolate muffins

These are divine. My daughters invite friends simply, I believe, so they can eat these wonderfully sinful but wholesome delights!

30g (1 oz) of butter
3 tablespoons of vanilla syrup
1 egg
4 tablespoons of full-fat milk
Punnet of strawberries
150g (5^1/$_2$ oz) of white chocolate
150g (5^1/$_2$ oz) of plain flour
1 teaspoon of baking powder
^{1}/$_2$ teaspoon of bicarbonate of soda
6 muffin cases

Leave the butter to melt in a bowl on the top of the Aga and mix with the vanilla syrup and egg. Chop the strawberries into quarters and enjoy smashing the chocolate into small pieces!

Mix the dry ingredients in a bowl, then add the butter, vanilla syrup, egg mixture and the milk. Add the chocolate and strawberries and gently mix until you have a deliciously lumpy mulch. Put the muffin cases into a muffin tray and spoon in the mixture. With the grid shelf on the floor of the roasting oven, put in the muffin tray and cook for about 25 minutes. If the muffins start to brown too quickly, slide in the cold plain shelf on the third set of runners. In a four oven Aga, place the muffin tray on the grid shelf on the third set of runners of the baking oven. Cook for about 25 minutes.

Makes 6 muffins

We had a gardener who refused to work unless he had a cup of coffee and one of these muffins!

cinnamon toast

Eating this on freezing winter mornings is an abiding memory.
In my teens, a group of us used to go to a little café in Hampstead
and eat endless rounds washed down with mugs of hot
chocolate....

2 thick slices of bread
Unsalted butter
$1/_2$ teaspoon of ground cinnamon
1 tablespoon of golden caster sugar

Cinnamon toast takes minutes to make.
My children all love it and I have found
them in the kitchen at some ungodly hour
making batches of it, ready for me to pop
in the Aga when I stagger downstairs.
It's blissful on cold winter mornings and
perfect as a bedtime treat. I have to
admit, I eat it at any time of day and it's
a good alternative to the plain variety.

Toast the bread on one side in the Aga
toaster. Butter the untoasted side. Mix the
cinnamon with the sugar and sprinkle it
on the buttered side of the toast.

Place the bread on a baking sheet,
buttered side up and hang on the highest
set of runners in the roasting oven.
Cook for about 30 seconds to one minute
or until the sugar has melted and has
started to bubble nicely.

Serves 1

Fabulously simple prepare-in-a-moment treats just
bursting with wonderful feelgood flavours....

seriously good smoothies

Not Aga recipes, I know, but too delicious to leave out.
Plus, they're so healthy you'll feel exceedingly smug having had
them for breakfast!

Juicy Smoothie
1 ripe banana
10 strawberries
1 ripe mango
250ml (9 fl oz) chilled fresh orange juice
Ice cubes

Peel the mango, removing the large stone
in the middle, and slice. Slice the banana
and cut the strawberries in half. Put all the
ingredients, including the orange juice,
into a blender and blitz until completely
smooth. Pour into glasses over ice. Enjoy!
Substitute vanilla soya milk for the orange
juice if you fancy a change.

Serves 1

Creamy Smoothie
75ml (2$^3/_4$ fl oz) of pineapple juice
170g (6 oz) of diced pineapple
1 chopped banana
Large scoop of vanilla ice cream
Ice cubes

Simply throw everything – including the
pineapple juice – into a blender and
whizz it up until completely smooth.
Then pour into glasses over ice and
enjoy the journey to more exotic climes.

Serves 1

smoked salmon blinis

My first boyfriend's mother, who was unbelievably glamorous, used to make these every Sunday morning and I can't eat them without being instantly transported back to her kitchen....

300ml (10 fl oz) of milk
6g sachet of easy-blend yeast
5ml (1 tsp) of sugar
25g (1 oz) of buckwheat flour
175g (7 oz) of strong plain flour
5ml (1 tsp) of salt
2 eggs, separated
25g (1 oz) of butter
600g (1 lb 5^1/$_2$ oz) of smoked salmon
300ml (10 fl oz) of soured cream
Chopped chives to garnish

Gently warm the milk in a pan on the simmering plate and blend with the yeast and sugar. Leave to stand for 10 minutes. Sieve the flours and salt into a mixing bowl and make a well in the centre. Gradually beat in the milk mixture and egg yolks.

Cover and leave in a warm place (on the simmering plate lid is a good place for this) for an hour.

Whisk the egg whites and fold into the batter. Lightly grease the simmering plate with butter. Spoon the mixture in tablespoons on to the simmering plate, leaving even spaces between them. Cook each side for 30 seconds.

Top each blini with smoked salmon and very cold soured cream. Garnish with chopped chives.

Makes about 12

Instead of the chives, try Avruga as a garnish...
the bold colours look really fantastic together.

ham and emmental croissants

Ham and Emmental are a perfect combination. The nuttiness of the cheese goes perfectly with the slight saltiness of the ham. Add that to the sweet flakiness of the croissant and you've culinary heaven.

1 slice of ham
1 fairly thick slice of Emmental
A good grind of black pepper
1 croissant

Sometimes when we're feeling really lazy on a Saturday morning we take the children out for breakfast to a fabulous café in Holt called Byfords.

Short of enjoying warm croissants and café au lait in Paris, they do the best we've had. Much better than the rubbery supermarket variety. Often, we buy a bag to bring home and on Sunday morning I'll fill them with ham and cheese and we'll eat them in the garden if the weather's being kind.

Split the croissant in two and put the ham on one side with the cheese on top. Grill that half of the croissant at the top of the roasting oven for a few minutes until the cheese has melted. It's important not to overdo them – they're undoubtedly best only lightly crisped with the cheese oozing out delightfully. Place the other half of the croissant in the oven for the last 30 seconds or so, then put the croissant back together again and enjoy!

For a cold filled croissant, try smoked salmon and cream cheese with a sprinkling of chives.

Serves 1

swiss-style frittata

This recipe is simple, filling and seriously wholesome, but it doesn't taste the least bit worthy.

4 potatoes, diced
$^1/_2$ an onion, sliced
1 tablespoon of vegetable oil
8 eggs, beaten
100g (3$^1/_2$ oz) of chopped ham
Salt and freshly ground pepper to taste
100g (3$^1/_2$ oz) of grated Emmental

On the boiling plate, bring to the boil a large pan of salted water. Add the potatoes and cook until they're tender but still firm. Drain and set aside to cool.

Heat the oil in a cast-iron frying pan on the simmering plate. Add the onions and cook slowly, stirring occasionally, until soft.

Stir in the eggs, potatoes, ham, salt and pepper. Cook until the eggs are firm.
Top the frittata with the grated cheese and put the pan into the roasting oven with the grid shelf on the second set of runners until the cheese has melted.

Serves 4

You can caramelise the onions and skip the ham.
Try these with Mozzarella and cherry tomatoes.

ciabatta with goats' cheese and mushrooms

Perfect for an informal brunch. It takes only 15 minutes to make and is fab with a huge bowl of salad and a large glass of dry white wine.

1 ciabatta loaf
60ml (2 fl oz) of olive oil
1 garlic clove, crushed
100g (3$^1/_2$ oz) creamy goats' cheese
60ml (2 fl oz) of sun-dried tomato paste
125g (4$^1/_2$ oz) of mushrooms,
   thinly sliced
Parsley, chopped

Cut the bread in half lengthways and then each piece in half again to make four slices. In a shallow bowl, mix the olive oil with the garlic. Press the cut side of the bread into the olive oil.

Spread each slice with the goats' cheese and the sun-dried tomato paste. Place on a baking tray and spoon over the mushrooms and the remaining oil. Cook in the roasting oven, with the grid shelf on the lowest set of runners, for about 10 minutes.

Serve immediately, garnished with parsley.

Serves 4

prawn savoury

I discovered this recipe in a charming booklet called *Menus and Recipes for Aga Cookery Demonstrations*, first published in 1939. It makes a lovely light brunch.

8 large prawns
8 fingers of toast
8 rashers of streaky bacon
Lemon juice
Seasoning

Shell the prawns and sprinkle with lemon juice and seasoning. Roll each prawn in a thin rasher of streaky bacon.

Lay them on a baking sheet and place them in the roasting oven for around 5–7 minutes.

Serve on fingers of hot buttered toast.

Serves 4

'This is a simple but effective dish that's so good served with drinks before dinner... total bliss!

brunch crêpes

These crêpes are like a mini-breakfast in their own right, but unusual enough to serve as a brunch for friends. Be sure to make enough though – they have a habit of disappearing quickly!

For the crêpes
125g (5 oz) of plain flour
Large pinch of of salt
2 eggs
250ml (8 fl oz) of milk
25g (1 oz) of melted butter
Vegetable oil

Sieve all the dry ingredients into a mixing bowl and make a well in the centre.
Add the eggs and half of the milk. Gradually mix together to make a smooth, thick batter. Stir in the remaining milk and the melted butter. Beat for 2–3 minutes. For each crêpe, heat 5ml of oil in a frying pan on the boiling plate until very hot and pour in a thin film of batter. Cook until it's a gorgeous golden colour, then flip over the crêpe and cook the other side. Keep it warm in the simmering oven while you make the other crêpes and the filling.

For the filling
1 egg fried to your liking
3 rashers of cooked bacon cut into
 small pieces
75g (3 oz) of diced sautéed potatoes
1 tbsp of parsley, chopped

To assemble
Place the crêpe on a warmed plate. Put the egg in the centre. Scatter the bacon and potatoes around the egg. Garnish with parsley.

Serves 6–8

egg and onion bagels

The staple ingredient of a deli breakfast, at home we pile the table with egg and onion, smoked salmon, cream cheese and smoked cod's roe and make up our bagels as we go along.

8 bagels
7 eggs
Five tablespoons of mayonnaise
Small bunch of spring onions, chopped
Salt and black pepper

Bring a pan of water on the boiling plate and, when it starts to bubble, move to the simmering plate and add the eggs. Leave to simmer for 8–10 minutes.

Remove the eggs from the pan and place in a bowl of ice cold water. When the eggs are cool enough, peel them. Mash the eggs in a bowl, adding the mayonnaise, spring onions, salt and pepper.

Lightly toast the split bagels using the Aga toaster on the simmering plate.

Then spread the egg and onion mixture on the bagel.

Serves 4

Pile the bagels high, serve with a huge bowl of egg and onion and let the good times roll....

ham and pepper piperade

This dish is an exquisite mix of soft scrambled eggs and slightly crunchy vegetables. The ham gives it a delicious, almost smoky quality.

150ml (5 fl oz) of olive oil (not extra virgin)
6 slices of Prosciutto ham
1 medium onion, finely chopped
3 ripe tomatoes, peeled and coarsely chopped
1 green pepper, cut into thin strips
1 red pepper, cut into thin strips
2 cloves of garlic, minced
8 fresh eggs
50ml (2 fl oz) of double cream
Salt and freshly ground pepper

Heat the oil in a large pan on the simmering plate and sauté the ham for about two minutes. Remove and put on a plate. Sauté the onions for about five minutes. Add the tomatoes, peppers, and garlic and cook gently until almost all the juices have evaporated.

Beat together the eggs and the cream, add the salt and pepper and pour over the vegetables in the pan.

Gently stir the eggs so they don't stiffen – they should be the texture of soft scrambled egg rather than that of an omelette.

Garnish with the ham before serving.

Serves 2–4

One of my newly discovered favourites.
Simply gorgeous with fresh crusty bread and a salad.

good food fast

a word about good food fast

If I could have more of anything, it would definitely be time. More time to spend with my children, my husband, my friends and myself! As time is precious and food is divine, I think it's important to have a stack of recipes that allow you to cook something delicious in minutes.

Simple dishes that can be cooked with the minimum of fuss, but still taste scrummy. I hate feeling so exhausted that I end up eating something that's a compromise. It's so unnecessary, particularly as good food can be so uplifting.

One of the biggest myths about the Aga is that you can only cook complicated dishes that take hours. This couldn't be further from the truth. Because the Aga's always ready you don't have to wait around for it to pre-heat. Instead, you can just throw the food in or on to it with the minimum of fuss.

I love sitting – tray on lap, glass in hand – watching an episode of *Sex and the City*. The local pizza company used to be one of my Friends and Family numbers until I discovered the unadulterated pleasure of whipping up home-made TV suppers. These are dishes you won't find served in a trendy restaurant, but they're utterly delicious and seriously cosseting.

I've also included some great ideas for times when friends drop in and you need to entertain in a hurry. There's no point getting frazzled: good friends don't expect Michelin-starred food! You might as well whip up simple dishes that take minutes and can be prepared while you're chatting over a glass of wine.

Cooking should be stress-free and enjoyable. The recipes here are deliberately loose, easy and, above all else, achievable.

aga fish and chips

Good fish and chips are unbeatable; bad fish and chips are utterly
unbearable. The Aga is perfect for cooking Britain's favourite dish
and you can even have it on a Sunday when the chippie's closed.

8 large, floury potatoes
2 tablespoons of organic sunflower oil
225g (8 oz) of self-raising flour
Pinch of garlic powder
300ml (10 fl oz) of lager (ideally organic)
Salt and white pepper
4 haddock fillets

I remember being utterly staggered
at how easy it is to make beer batter.
Really, it's easier than pancakes.

Cut the potatoes into chips. Cover in a
healthy sprinkling of sunflower oil and place
on a baking tray on the floor of the roasting
oven for 30–40 minutes. Set aside a
couple of spoonfuls of flour and mix with
the garlic powder. Mix the rest of the
flour, lager, salt and pepper in a mixer.
The batter should be thick and gloopy –
if it feels too thin add some more flour.
Dip the cod in the flour and then the batter.
In a large frying pan, heat 1cm ($1/2$ in) of
oil until it's smoking. Add the fish to the
pan and cook for a few minutes until the
batter turns golden. Carefully lift out the
fish and place it on a baking sheet.
Put it on the grid shelf on the third set
of runners in the roasting oven and cook
for a further 10–15 minutes.

Serves 4

This batter is perfect with the meatiness of the haddock,
but can be used with other fish

home-made burger

I just love burgers. I realised how far my addiction had gone when, in a gorgeous Parisian restaurant with seriously luxurious food on the menu, I chose a burger from the children's section!

400g (14 oz) of organic minced beef
1 medium onion, finely chopped
1 egg
Large handful of fresh breadcrumbs
2 tablespoons of coriander, chopped
2 tablespoons of fresh chives, chopped
Tablespoon of tomato ketchup
Salt and ground black pepper

4 burger buns
4 large lettuce leaves
1 large tomato
4 slices of good Cheddar cheese

In a bowl, combine all the ingredients from the first set, adding the breadcrumbs as required. Mould the mixture into burger shapes – they can be as round or flat as you like.

Place the grill rack in the large roasting tin and put the burgers on top. Place it in the roasting oven on the third set of runners and cook for 20–25 minutes, according to your taste.

Cut the burger buns in half. Pop in the burger on top of the salad, add a slice of cheese and put the top on. Serve on their own or with chips.

Serves 4

A burger in a bun – my kind of haute cuisine!

best-ever baked potatoes

This is barely a recipe, more a reminder of just how fab good baked potatoes can be and a few suggestions as to how they might be served.

Prick the potatoes with a fork. Pop the potatoes on the grid shelf on the middle set of runners in the roasting oven. They'll take 60–90 minutes. When they're done take them out, cut them in half and worry the middle a little with a fork before smothering them in butter.

Pizza Spuds

My children like them topped like pizzas, with a little tomato purée, oregano and Mozzarella. Simply halve the potatoes, smear on the tomato purée, sprinkle on the herbs, pop on the cheese and stick the potatoes in a roasting tin in the roasting oven for about 7 minutes.

Tuna and Mayo

Mix a small tin of tuna with a dollop of mayonnaise and a good grind of pepper.

Soured Cream and Bacon Bits

Instead of butter, use soured cream with chopped chives. Fry small pieces of bacon in a little oil for a fab bacon bits topping.

Savoury Cheese

Pop grated Cheddar on top of the potato halves with a splash of Worcestershire sauce. Place them in a roasting tin and put them in the roasting oven (middle set of runners) for about 5 minutes or until the cheese starts to bubble and brown.

I can't eat these without thinking of Fireworks Night. I can almost smell the sulphur in the air.

unorthodox omelette

Omelette experts would probably baulk at this recipe, but it tastes great, takes minutes and shouldn't require any shopping. We often have it for lunch while we're working.

Butter, for frying
4 eggs
1 tablespoon of double cream
2 tablespoons of chives, chopped
Salt and freshly ground black pepper
2 tablespoons of grated Cheddar

Heat the butter in a heavy pan on the simmering plate. Put the eggs into a bowl and gently worry them a bit. This is different to frantic beating or enthusiastic whisking; it's gentler and will stop the omelette tasting at all rubbery. Add the cream, chives, salt and pepper.

When the butter starts to foam, oosh it about a bit so it covers the entire base of the pan and pour in the egg mixture.

As the egg begins to set, gently prise the corners away from the side of the pan and sprinkle on the cheese, ensuring it covers the whole omelette. Continue cooking until the omelette is just about set – the underneath should be a slightly golden colour and the cheese melted.

Tip the pan and fold the omelette in half. If you're sharing it, cut it in half at this point and serve on to a plate with buttered bread and some salad.

Serves 1–2

Be gentle with your omelette mix – too much beating can knock all the fluffiness out of it.

parmesan chicken

This chicken tastes so good and takes minutes to make. I love it with green beans and broccoli – it feels so virtuous!

**8 tablespoons of freshly grated
   Parmesan**
Pinch of black pepper
1 egg, beaten
4 skinned, boneless chicken breasts
Tablespoon of olive oil
Tablespoon of butter

Mix together the Parmesan and pepper. Brush the chicken breasts with the egg, then dip them in the Parmesan mixture.

Put the olive oil and the butter into a large, heavy-bottomed, oven-proof pan.

Heat it on the boiling plate for a minute or so. Pop in the chicken, turning it after a minute or two, and then cook on the other side. Move the pan to the floor of the roasting oven and cook until it's ready, turning the chicken once. This will probably take 5–7 minutes, depending on the thickness of the chicken breasts.

You can serve with this with chips, potato salad, a crisp green salad or fine green beans and broccoli. Scrummy.

Serves 2–4

The combination of Parmesan and black pepper lend this dish a deliciously crisp finish.

chicken and pepper pitta bread

You can, of course, fill pitta bread with anything you like, but I like it best like this. The onions caramelise beautifully and the chicken and peppers work particularly well together.

Tablespoon of butter
Tablespoon of olive oil
1 large onion, chopped
1 red pepper, sliced
1 green pepper, sliced
1 yellow pepper, sliced
4 chicken breasts, sliced
4 pieces of pitta bread
Soured cream

Heat the butter and olive oil in a large, flat-bottomed pan on the simmering plate. Place the onions in the pan and cook for a few minutes. When the onions have started to caramelise, add the peppers and continue to cook for another 5 minutes. Toss in the chicken and stir it around so it gets covered in the pan juices.

Cook for a further 10–15 minutes, ensuring the chicken is cooked through. Meanwhile, warm the pitta bread in the roasting oven for a minute or so. Cut it open and fill with the chicken and vegetables.

Top with the soured cream and enjoy!

Serves 4

sausages and mash in onion gravy

There are few things that conjure up childhood as effectively. The mash is the perfect foil to the richness of the sausages and gravy.

Butter
6 plump sausages
2 medium onions
Tablespoon of flour
$1/_2$ glass of red wine
150ml (5 fl oz) of hot stock
6 large potatoes
Tablespoon of double cream
Freshly ground black pepper

Melt the butter in a roasting tin on the simmering plate. Add the sausages and let them cook gently, turning occasionally. Chop the onions and add them to the roasting tin. Transfer the tin to the second set of runners in the roasting oven. Leave them for about 15 minutes until the onions are soft and the sausages cooked.

While the sausages are cooking, peel the potatoes and cut them into quarters. Bring them to the boil in a large pan on the boiling plate. Remove the sausages and keep them warm at the back of the Aga or in the simmering oven. Transfer the tin to the simmering plate and add the flour. After a minute, add the red wine and stock. Allow it to bubble on the simmering plate, stirring occasionally until you have a thick gravy. Drain and mash the potatoes with some butter, the cream and pepper.

Serves 4

The creamy mash contrasts wonderfully to the rich, savoury sausages and onion gravy.

pasta with tomato sauce

When I left home I did so armed with my record collection, an assortment of questionable clothes and this recipe. While my taste in music and fashion has moved on, I still cook this all the time.

2 x 400g (14 oz) tins of
   plum tomatoes
1 teaspoon of olive oil
1 clove of garlic, crushed
1 large onion, chopped
$1/_2$ teaspoon of sun-dried
   tomato purée
$1/_2$ glass of red wine
Small handful of fresh basil leaves,
   chopped
Maldon salt and freshly ground black
   pepper
1 packet of pasta of your choice
Freshly grated Parmesan

Heat the oil in a large pan on the simmering plate. Add the onion and garlic and cook until they're soft. Roughly chop the tomatoes and add them, their juice, the wine, the basil, tomato purée, salt and pepper to the pan and move to the boiling plate. Bring to the boil. Cover the pan and move it to the simmering oven for 20 minutes. Cook the pasta in a large pan of salted water. Drain the pasta and serve. Take the pan with the sauce out of the simmering oven and spoon the sauce over the pasta. Sprinkle with grated Parmesan and serve with garlic bread.

Serves 2–4

ridiculously easy pasta

Sometimes, after a hard day, all I want is a big bowl of comforting blandness. When my mouth hurts from smiling and I'm incapable of uttering another word, I crave this deliriously cosseting pasta dish.

1 small packet of fresh spaghetti
1 clove of garlic, crushed
2 tablespoons of butter
4 rashers of bacon, chopped
Handful of freshly grated Parmesan
Black pepper

Bring a large pan of salted water to the boil on the boiling plate. Add the pasta and bring back to the boil. Move to the simmering plate and cook according to the manufacturer's instructions.

Melt the butter in a large pan on the boiling plate. Don't allow it to burn – just to froth nicely. Add the garlic and bacon and cook for a couple of minutes until the garlic is soft and the bacon is slightly crispy.

Take the pan off the heat. Drain the pasta and add it to the pan with the bacon and garlic. Stir it around so it becomes coated in the butter and bacon fat.

Add the Parmesan and put the pan back on the simmering plate for a minute or so. Then add the black pepper and serve the pasta in large bowls.

Serves 2

The ultimate fast-food dish... ready in moments and yet bursting with bright, natural flavours.

pork with garlic and rosemary

It seems like an overstatement to call this a recipe. But the humble pork chop is often forgotten, so I see it as a reminder. They take minutes to cook and really are perfect for lazy nights in.

1 large sprig of rosemary
2 large cloves of garlic
Maldon salt and a good grind of black pepper
Olive oil
1 teaspoon of crushed juniper berries
2 pork chops

Take the rosemary off the stalk and chop the garlic into tiny pieces. Add to a bowl along with the olive oil, juniper berries, salt and black pepper. Mix them together and then smear the mix over the chops.

Put a grill pan on the boiling plate and allow it to heat up for a minute or so. Place the chops in the pan. Cook them for two minutes or so, then turn them over and cook for another couple of minutes. Move the pan to the simmering plate and leave it there for about 5 minutes.

Turn the chops over to cook the other side for another five-or-so minutes.

To check if they're done, make a small incision in the middle – if they're at all pink they're not done and should be left for a few more minutes.

Serves 2

chicken with mozzarella wrapped in ham

This has a certain country house hotel kitsch, but tastes fab and is perfect when you've just got in from work and have friends to feed.

2 balls of Mozzarella
4 skinned, boneless chicken breasts
8 slices of cured ham

I can't remember the first time I had ham and Mozzarella with chicken, but there's something about the combination that makes it truly wonderful. I first cooked it when I'd forgotten we had friends coming for dinner and it was an instant hit.

Slice the Mozzarella. Fry over the chicken until it's golden on both sides. Take it out of the pan and make an incision in the fleshiest part in the middle. Stuff the Mozzarella into the chicken and wrap slices of ham around each breast.

Transfer the chicken to an oven-proof dish and bake in the roasting oven, with the grid shelf on the lowest set of runners, for about 15 minutes.

Check the chicken is cooked through by cutting into it and making sure you can see no pink.

Serves 4

glazed steaks

If I'm feeling tired or stressed, all I crave is a seriously bloody steak and a huge plate of chips. The Aga is perfect – allowing the meat to sit in the simmering oven ensures it's beautifully butter-soft.

4 tablespoons of toasted sesame oil
4 tablespoons of soy sauce
Salt and freshly ground black pepper
4 fillet steaks

Mix the sesame oil with the soy sauce, salt and pepper in a shallow bowl. Pop the steaks in and marinate for a few minutes.

Meanwhile, place a ridged grill pan on the boiling plate and allow it to get really hot. Place the steaks in the pan and allow them to cook for only a minute or so on each side. You want them to have lovely ridges from the pan, but not to get overdone in the slightest.

Remove the steaks from the pan, put them in an ovenproof dish and transfer them to the simmering oven for 5 or so minutes, depending on how you like them cooked.

Serve with a crisp salad in summer or a bowl of creamy mashed potato and fine green beans in the winter.

Serves 4

A really good steak is hard to beat...
the Aga's radiant heat positively locks in all the flavour.

seared lamb fillets

Simple but effective, which is what emergency food is all about. You can't go wrong with this dish. It was one of the first things I cooked with an Aga and it shows how fab the simmering oven is.

Tablespoon of sesame oil
4 thick lamb fillets
Salt and pepper

On the boiling plate, heat the oil in a large, heavy bottomed pan. Season the lamb fillets with the salt and pepper and place them in the pan. Leave them for about 5 minutes before turning them over and cooking the other side for the same amount of time.

Take the lamb out of the pan and put in an oven-proof dish. Place in the roasting oven for another 5–10 minutes, depending on how pink you like your lamb.

Cut into slices and arrange on warmed plates.

Serve with a big salad, creamy garlic potatoes (see page 49) and crusty bread.

Serves 4

creamy garlicky potatoes

If I could only eat potatoes one way it would be like this.
The soft potato swimming in garlic-infused cream is so divinely
delicious it's difficult to imagine any potato dish surpassing it.

1kg (2^1/$_4$ lb) of potatoes
2 really fat cloves of garlic
Butter, to grease the dish
600ml (20 fl oz) of double cream
Salt and freshly ground black pepper

While this isn't the quickest dish to cook,
it takes little preparation and needs only
the most perfunctory of glances to make
sure it's not browning too quickly. If it is,
either cover the dish with foil – removing
it for the last 10 minutes or so – or slide
the cold plain shelf in above it.

Peel and thinly slice the potatoes. Slice
the garlic. Grease the baking dish with a
seriously generous amount of butter.
Arrange the potatoes and garlic, in layers,
in the dish, seasoning with the salt and
pepper as you go along. Once they're
all in, pour in the cream so that it almost
covers the potatoes.

With the grid shelf on the floor of the
roasting oven, slide in the dish and cook
for between 1 and 1^1/$_2$ hours.

Serves 2 as a main dish

*Melt-in-the-mouth gorgeousness... the perfect
accompaniment to any red meat or white fish.*

asparagus and parmesan risotto

The creamy consistency of the rice and the clean taste of the asparagus make this dish. Serve it with a bowl of salad and bread. Perfect on the sofa or as informal food for friends.

Tablespoon of butter
1 onion, finely chopped
2 cloves of garlic, crushed
320g (11^1/$_4$ oz) of Arborio rice
1 glass of dry white wine
1 litre of hot chicken or vegetable stock
1 tablespoon of butter
Freshly grated Parmesan

In a heavy bottomed oven-proof pan sauté the onion and garlic. Cook on the simmering plate for about 5 minutes.

Add the asparagus, then the rice and mix well until it's coated and cook until it's utterly transparent. Add the wine and stir until it's evaporated or been absorbed.

Move the pan to the boiling plate and add the stock and bring to the boil. Transfer it to the floor of the simmering oven and leave for around 20 minutes.

Check all the liquid has been absorbed and that the rice is tender and creamy, but still firm to the bite. Stir in the butter and Parmesan.

Serves 4

Totally ideal for cuddle-up evenings or when a group of friends drop by unexpectedly.

swordfish with tomato and basil salad

Swordfish is best not messed around with too much. The meaty flesh of the fish tastes so yummy I prefer to cook it very simply.

4 x 170g (6oz) swordfish steaks
Olive oil
Maldon salt and freshly ground
   black pepper
8 beef tomatoes
Handful of basil leaves

If you're cooking for friends and are in a hurry, this dish is perfect because it takes only about 10 minutes to prepare

Rub the swordfish steaks with a little olive oil and the salt and pepper. On the boiling plate, heat a ridged grill pan. When it's seriously hot, place the swordfish steaks in and cook for about 2 minutes on each side. Meanwhile, slice the tomatoes relatively thinly and arrange on the plates with the basil leaves. Drizzle over a little olive oil and grind some black pepper over them.

When the swordfish is cooked, serve it on the plates with the salad.

Serves 4

haddock with lemon and coriander

This tastes so clean and fresh that eating it makes one feel virtuous. There's something about good fish cooked well and treated simply that really brings out the taste of the sea.

2 tablespoons of lemon rind, freshly grated
2 tablespoons of flat-leaf parsley, chopped
2 tablespoons of coriander, chopped
Maldon salt and freshly ground black pepper
4 haddock fillets
Olive oil

I love buying fresh fish from my local fishmonger. Don't you find the colourful displays of the day's catch simply invite one to cook?

And don't be bashful about asking to inspect any fish you fancy – there should be no discernible odour and the eyes should be bright and vivid; not at all dull.

In a shallow bowl, mix together the lemon rind, parsley, coriander, olive oil, salt and pepper. Press each piece of fish into the mixture, ensuring it's well coated on both sides. Heat the olive oil in a large frying pan on the boiling plate. Cook the fish for a few minutes on each side, ensuring it's cooked through.

Serve with fresh vegetables and new potatoes.

Serves 4

scallops with pasta

Scallops are probably the easiest things to cook, but for some reason people imagine they'll be complicated. Because of this they always feel a bit posh and so are perfect as food for friends.

1 large packet of tagliatelle
100g (3$^1/_2$ oz) of butter
16 scallops
2 fat cloves of garlic, very finely
 chopped

On the boiling plate, bring a pan of water to the boil and put in the pasta. Bring back to the boil, move the pan to the simmering plate and cook the pasta according to the instructions on the packet.

Melt the butter in a large frying pan on the boiling plate until it starts to bubble. Add the garlic and cook for about 2 minutes. Then add the scallops to the pan and cook for a further 2 minutes. Turn over the scallops to cook on the other side for another couple of minutes.

Drain the pasta and put it on to warm plates. Top with the scallops, then pour over some of the garlicky butter sauce. Serve with thick bread for mopping up.

Serves 4

tiger prawn salad

Another dish that takes little time to prepare and is perfect for lazy summer suppers. My favourite evenings are spent in the garden chatting, drinking good wine and eating this kind of effortless salad.

Salt and freshly ground black pepper
16 raw tiger prawns, shelled
100g (3$^1/_2$ oz) of butter
2 fat cloves of garlic, very finely chopped
Large bag of salad leaves
2 large tomatoes, sliced
2 avocados
Salad dressing of your choice

Season the prawns with the salt and pepper. On the boiling plate, melt the butter in a large frying pan until it starts to bubble. Add the garlic and cook for 2 minutes, then add the prawns to the pan and cook for a further few minutes, stirring the prawns around. How long the prawns take depends on how plump they are. They're done when they have turned from grey to a glorious pink.

Arrange the salad leaves, tomatoes and avocado on plates and top with the just-cooked prawns. Pour over the dressing and enjoy!

Serves 4

This magical combination of colours and flavours would also work really well with scallops

lime and coriander prawns

Not a huge supper by any means, but perfect for summer evenings. You could, of course, serve this as a first course and have pasta or something to follow. But we usually have this and then a pudding.

16 large tiger prawns
2 cloves of garlic, peeled and crushed
6 tablespoons of butter
1 tablespoon of coriander, finely
   chopped
Maldon salt and black pepper
5 limes

Peel the prawns, but leave the tails intact, then cut down the centre of each prawn and ease it open and remove the vein that runs down the middle. Open out each prawn and flatten it. Then rinse them under a cold tap.

Mix the butter, garlic and coriander in a bowl. Put the prawns in a roasting tin lined with Bake-O-Glide and smear on the butter mixture. Sprinkle with the salt and pepper and slide the roasting tin on to the middle set of runners in the roasting oven. Cook for about 6 minutes.

Put the prawns on plates and squeeze over a little lime juice.

Serve with lime wedges, fresh crusty bread and a bowl of crisp green salad.

Serves 4

Two beautiful flavours that together really sing.

new potato salad

If you're called upon to provide food for friends, this potato salad is a great stand-by – we often have a bowl in the fridge and dip into it on an all too regular basis. It can be served warm or cold.

500g (1 lb 2 oz) of Charlotte potatoes
3 large tablespoons of mayonnaise
Small bunch of spring onions, chopped
Salt and black pepper

Good potato salad is a real pleasure – the contrast between the waxy potato and the creamy mayonnaise is sublime.

You can add anything you like, of course – I like spring onions or chopped chives.

On the boiling plate, place the whole potatoes in a pan of cold salted water. Bring them to the boil and allow them to bubble away for 15–20 minutes until they're still firm and not falling apart, but are soft in the middle.

If necessary, chop the potatoes. Then put the potatoes in a bowl, add the mayonnaise, spring onions, salt and pepper and give it a good mix. That's it: simple, but scrummy!

Makes 1 large bowl

cooking for kids

a word about cooking for kids

There are few things in the world as lovely as a few hours spent in the kitchen with children. Forget shopping for wildly expensive shoes or being pampered to within an inch of your life. A lovely happy child covered in flour and chattering away while enjoying one of life's most basic pleasures is, for me at least, time sent from heaven.

I believe the most important thing about entertaining children in the kitchen is to make it fun. They spend so much time engaged in high-tech pursuits that something as simple as licking a spoonful of deliciously gooey cake mixture can seem to them so marvellous.

The recipes in this section are things we eat all the time. They're also recipes that I've cooked with all my children. Many of them make a quick weekday supper or after-school snack.

Sometimes when I'm cooking I can't move for children wanting to help, while at other times they'd far rather get on with something else and leave the work to me. Whatever their mood, I love having them in the kitchen with me – learning to cook and becoming familiar with food is one of life's most basic skills and best learned in the kitchen at home.

An Aga kitchen is the heart of the home,
a place where memories are made.
There are few things a parent remembers
as tear-jerkingly vividly as their child
proudly showing off something they've
made themselves or hearing that
wonderful phrase 'my mummy makes the
best...' I believe no child should enter their
teenage years without having made
at least one batch of fairy cakes or having
subjected his parents to a truly hideous
meal that he's made 'especially for them'.

So enjoy cooking these recipes with your
children. Involve them and indulge them
and I guarantee you'll have delicious fun.

aga cheese on toast

There's something about this ridiculously simple dish cooked in an Aga that makes it taste absolutely blissful. It's the perfect tea-time treat for children – it takes minutes and is packed full of protein.

1 slice of Cheddar cheese
1 slice of Red Leicester
2 slices of white bread
1 slice of streaky bacon

If you were to butter the bread before putting on the cheese, this recipe would be a version of Scotch Rabbit, slightly more child-friendly than its Welsh counterpart. I absolutely refuse to call it 'rarebit', since I firmly believe that name was conjured up by people who feel the need to make language more complicated than it should be. The fact is that since the early 18th century cooks have been writing about Welsh Rabbit, so that's how it should stay!

There's something about the way the bacon melts into the cheese that gives it a deliciously salty taste.

Cut the cheese into inch-wide (2.5cm) strips and place on the bread, alternating the cheeses so you end up with stripes. Cut the bacon into little pieces and sprinkle on top.

Cook on a baking sheet on the floor of the roasting oven for about six minutes. The bread will toast underneath, so there's no need to toast it first.

Serve with a crisp green salad and, if you like them, some plain potato crisps.

Serves 1

croque monsieur

Quick and easy – the problem is avoiding eating it before it makes it on to your child's plate. If your children don't like ham, you can simply substitute tomatoes.

1 egg
Splash of full-fat milk
Freshly ground black pepper
A little soft butter
4 thick slices of bread
2 slices of ham
2 slices of Emmental

In a shallow bowl, beat the egg, adding a little milk and pepper. Butter the bread on one side. Put the ham and cheese between the bread on the buttered side and press each made-up sandwich into the eggy mixture in the bowl.

Heat a cast-iron frying pan on the simmering plate for a couple of minutes. Place each sandwich in the pan.

Cook for a couple of minutes until the underneath is a gorgeous golden colour and the cheese has started to melt.

Flip the sandwich over in the pan and cook the other side for a couple of minutes.

Take the sandwich out of the pan and cut it into quarters. Then serve and watch it disappear!

Serves 2 – but they won't stop at that!

My youngest son would only get on the Eurostar once he was told this dish originated in France

simple banana bread

A true taste of childhood and wonderful warm or cold, banana bread is so delicious that it disappears almost as soon as it's baked. Spread it with lashings of unsalted butter and wait for the rush.

125g (4$^1/_2$ oz) of soft butter
125g (4$^1/_2$ oz) of golden caster sugar
2 eggs
1 teaspoon of vanilla extract
4 large bananas
175g (6 oz) of plain flour
Pinch of salt
$^1/_2$ teaspoon of bicarbonate of soda
2 teaspoons of baking powder
3 tablespoons of full-fat milk
900g (2 lb) loaf tin

Having children who are almost pathologically afraid of 'bits', my banana bread contains no sultanas, raisins or nuts, although you should feel free to add them if you want to.

Mix the butter and sugar together in a bowl. Add the eggs and vanilla extract and continue mixing until smooth. Mash the bananas and add them to the mix. Then slowly add the flour, salt, bicarbonate of soda, milk and baking powder. Grease and line a loaf tin and pour in the mixture. For a two-oven Aga, put the grid shelf on the floor of the roasting oven with the cold, plain shelf on the second set of runners. For a three-oven or four-oven Aga, put the grid shelf on the lowest set of runners in the baking oven and slide in the tin. Bake for about 45 minutes.

Makes one loaf

A firm favourite that disappears at great speed!
It's lovely warm and spread thickly with butter

chocolate and banana toastie

Banana and chocolate is a perfect combination. Remember those chocolate-coated banana sweets sold alongside lurid pink shrimps and sugar mice with string tails? This is the sandwich equivalent.

1 ripe banana
1 teaspoon of full-fat milk
Healthy dollop of Green & Black's
   chocolate spread
Butter for spreading
4 slices of thick white bread

For years I had an aversion to banana sandwiches, remembering – with a shudder – soggy offerings packed in Tupperware and reluctantly eaten at the back of the school bus.

However, my youngest son has always adored bananas (and chocolate come to that), and this sandwich came about as a way to persuade him to eat something he could pick up himself when he was tiny.

In a bowl, mash the banana with the milk. Spread one side of each slice of the bread with a little butter and then the chocolate spread. Then spread the banana mixture on one side and make into sandwiches.

Put the sandwiches in the Aga toaster and place them on the simmering plate, with the lid down, for a couple of minutes on each side.

Makes two sandwiches

Grab the children, take the phone off the hook and eat these up while no one's looking!

classic tuna melt

This classic couldn't be simpler. Served with a salad, it makes a quick and easy supper for those days when you're frantic. You can, of course, use any bread you happen to have around.

Small tin of tuna
1 tablespoon of mayonnaise
2 slices of ciabatta
2 thin slices of Gruyère

Most children like tuna. It's good for them and a perfect store cupboard basic, making the Tuna Melt a real winner. You can do all sorts of things to spice it up, including adding a splash of Worcestershire sauce, a couple of anchovies or even some fried onions.

Mix the tuna and mayonnaise together. Spread on the ciabatta. Top with the cheese and place on a baking sheet. Put the baking sheet on the floor of the roasting oven and cook for a few minutes. Then move it to the top of the roasting oven and cook until the cheese starts to bubble.

Serve with a crisp green salad.

Makes enough for one

ice cream parlour milk shake

My daughters, Lucie and Tatti, invented this drink while messing around in the kitchen one day. It was the result of a tussle over a packet of Maltesers and it tastes almost too scrummy.

1 scoop of vanilla ice cream
$^1/_2$ pint (10 fl oz) of full-fat milk
1 packet of Maltesers
1 banana
1 tablespoon of chocolate syrup
4 mini marshmallows

When Whiteleys in Bayswater was newly opened and my eldest daughter was very small, I used to sneak off there and hang out in the ice cream parlour drinking chocolate malts, with her babbling away to herself in her pram.

From that moment on she was a bit of a milk shake fiend and still adores them to this day.

Chop the bananas into small pieces and place them, along with everything else except the marshmallows and Maltesers, into the blender.

Blitz for about a minute-and-a-half, then pour into a tall glass.

Smash the Maltesers to smithereens (all children love this bit!) and pour them into the glass. Give it a stir with a swizzle stick or long spoon and top with the mini marshmallows.

Makes one sinful glass

Perfect for sleepovers, parties or days with a 'Y'

chilli chocolate wraps

Don't baulk at the idea of these for kids. While the chilli kicks, it's not overpowering and the novelty value of the cocoa powder appeals to most children's sense of the ridiculous and adds depth.

1 tablespoon of olive oil
2 onions, finely chopped
3 fat cloves of garlic, finely chopped
450g (14^1/$_2$ oz) of best minced beef
1 teaspoon of crushed cumin seeds
2 400g tins of plum tomatoes
2 tablespoons of sun-dried tomato paste
1 teaspoon of chilli powder
1 teaspoon of cocoa powder (I prefer Green & Black's)
Freshly ground black pepper and salt
8 soft tortillas
50g (1^1/$_2$ oz) of Parmesan, grated
Small tub of soured cream
Handful of fresh coriander leaves
1 fresh lime

On the simmering plate, heat the olive oil in a large oven-proof pan or casserole with a lid. Fry the onions and garlic. Add the mince; fry until brown. Add the cumin seeds. Pour in the tomatoes and chop them in the pan. Add the tomato paste, chilli and cocoa powder and stir. Add salt and pepper and cover the pan. Transfer it to the simmering oven for 1–2 hours.

Wrap the tortillas in foil and heat in the roasting oven for about 5 minutes. Place two good tablespoons of the chilli mix in each tortilla, then add some Parmesan, a good dollop of soured cream and fresh coriander leaves. Roll the tortillas and serve with lime wedges.

Serves 2

pizza-topped baked potatoes

My children are pizza obsessed – they love the lovely stringy Mozzarella. They also like baked potatoes, so this is the perfect combination. You can add extra toppings, but I prefer them like this.

2 large potatoes
3 large ripe vine tomatoes
Teaspoon of olive oil
$^1/_2$ teaspoon of sun-dried tomato purée
Sprinkling of dried oregano
Tiny pinch of salt
Freshly ground black pepper
1 Mozzarella cheese

Cut the potatoes in half and put them on a rack in a roasting tin and bake in the roasting oven, with the grid shelf on the bottom set of runners, for around 45 minutes, depending on the size.

Pop the tomatoes in a bowl of boiling water for a couple of minutes. Take the bowl to the sink and leave it under the running tap until the tomatoes have cooled. Peel the skins with a sharp knife, then blitz them in a blender. In a bowl, mix together the tomatoes, olive oil, tomato purée, oregano, salt and pepper.

When the potatoes are done, take them out of the Aga and spread the tomato mixture on them. Slice the Mozzarella and place on the top. Pop the roasting tin back in the Aga, as high as it will go, and leave for about 5 minutes. Check the cheese has browned and is bubbly; if not, pop them back in for another couple of minutes.

Serve with salad, or as my children prefer, Heinz Spaghetti!

Serves 4

Two favourites in one. What could be better?

robbie's sausage surprise

This recipe was created by Robbie, the son of a friend, for a
Year 9 pasta project. It's perfect for children to cook and is
a fantastic weekday supper that's also ridiculously easy to make.

4 thick pork sausages
200g (8 oz) of coloured pasta
1 tablespoon of vegetable oil
1 red pepper, sliced
1 onion, sliced
100g (4 oz) of mushrooms, sliced
200g (8 oz) tin of sweetcorn
400g (16 oz) tin of chopped tomatoes
Pinch of dried mixed herbs
Salt and pepper
100g (4 oz) of Mozzarella, sliced

Place the sausages on the rack of the
small Aga roasting tin and hang on the
top set of runners in the roasting oven
and cook until done.

Cook the pasta in boiling, salted water for
10 minutes, or according to the instructions
on the packet. Drain well and set aside.

Fry the onion and pepper in oil in a large
frying pan for about 5 minutes. Add the
mushrooms and fry for 1 minute. Stir in the
sweetcorn, tomatoes, herbs and seasoning.

Slice each sausage into 8 and add to the
pan. Place the cooked pasta in the pan and
mix everything together. Put everything in
an ovenproof dish and top with Mozzarella.
Place on the grid shelf on the floor of the
roasting oven for 5–10 minutes until the
cheese has melted and started to brown.

Serve with garlic bread.

Serves 4

If only all school work tasted so good!

individual toad-in-the-hole

Jack, who's seven, was absolutely enraptured the first time I made this for him. A big fan of sausages, his delight that something different could be done with them was palpable.

Butter, for greasing
6 chipolatas
125g (4^1/$_2$ oz) of plain flour
2 large eggs
150ml (5 fl oz) of milk
Muffin tray with six spaces

Lightly grease the muffin tray and place one chipolata in each hole. Cook on the floor of the roasting oven for 3 minutes.

Take it out and turn the chipolatas over. Then put it back in for another couple of minutes.

While it's cooking, put the flour into a bowl, make a well in the middle and stir in the eggs. Gradually add the milk, until you have a smooth batter. Add the salt and pepper. Alternatively, you can simply throw everything into a mixer and whiz for a few minutes.

Take the muffin tray out of the Aga, pour the batter over the sausages and put back in the roasting oven, on the third set of runners, for about 15 minutes.

Serve with salad, broccoli and cauliflower – or Heinz Baked Beans!

Makes 6

parmesan-coated chicken strips

These are such a good alternative to frozen chicken nuggets and they only take a few minutes longer. The coating can also be used on whole chicken breasts for a fab chicken sandwich.

2 skinned, boneless chicken breasts
1 egg
2 tablespoons of Parmesan
3 tablespoons of breadcrumbs
Pinch of cayenne or black pepper

I like to use organic, corn-fed chicken for this recipe as I think the succulent flavour of the chicken works well with the slightly crunchy coating.

My boys are great fans of turkey dinosaurs – regarding them as the height of culinary indulgence – so I occasionally use this coating for turkey escallops, though I suspect they would still prefer them in the shape of a T-Rex!

Cut the chicken into strips, then break the egg into a small bowl and whisk a little. Brush the chicken with the egg. Mix together the Parmesan, breadcrumbs and pepper. Dip the chicken in the mixture. Place the chicken on a baking sheet, lined with Bake-O-Glide and put it on the floor of the roasting oven. Cook for about 15 minutes, turning the chicken over halfway through.

Children love these best with a pile of home-made Aga oven chips (see page 48 for the recipe).

Serves 2

perfect fish supper

This is so reminiscent of my own childhood suppers that I often eat it if I'm feeling miserable or am battling a deadline. The children love it as it's both comforting and easy to eat when they're tired.

4 large potatoes
Tablespoon of olive oil
Butter
2 thick pieces of haddock
Maldon salt
Freshly ground black pepper
4 tablespoons of double cream

Boil a pan of water on the boiling plate. Peel the potatoes (and cut in half if you think they may be too large). Drop them into the water and cook until tender.

While this is going on, heat the olive oil in a cast-iron frying pan on the simmering plate. Then add a tablespoon of butter. When it starts to bubble, carefully place the fish in the pan and leave it for a minute or two. Delicately turn over the fish and do the same on the other side. Sprinkle over the salt and black pepper and transfer the pan to the roasting oven.

The grid shelf should be on the floor; place the pan on to it. Leave it there for 6–8 minutes, checking it doesn't get overdone.

Drain the potatoes and mash them. Beat in a tablespoon of butter and the cream, adding a pinch of salt and the black pepper as you go.

Serve with lots of freshly buttered bread.

Serves 2

I cook this dish when I'm feeling a bit grumpy...
or the whole world seems to be against me!

creamy carbonara

Purists might turn their noses up at cream in a carbonara, but I think it gives it wonderful depth and the children adore it.

1 packet of bacon (about 6 rashers)
1 tablespoon of olive oil
6 tablespoons of white wine
1 packet of fresh spaghetti
6 egg yolks
6 tablespoons of double cream
40g (1^1/$_2$ oz) of freshly grated
    Parmesan
Black pepper
1 tablespoon of butter

Put a huge pan of water, with lots of salt, on to the boiling plate. Cut the bacon into smallish pieces and fry slowly in a large pan on the simmering plate, with the olive oil and a little butter. When the bacon starts to get crispy, add the wine to the pan and let it cook for a few minutes. Remove the pan from the heat and set it aside until everything else is ready.

Once the water has boiled, add the pasta and cook according to the instructions. Mix together the egg yolks, cream, Parmesan and black pepper.

When the pasta is ready, put the bacon back on the simmering plate and drain the spaghetti. Turn the spaghetti into the pan with the bacon. Oosh it around a bit and then remove from the heat. Add the eggy, cheesy mix and allow it to stand either on top of the simmering plate lid or close to the Aga.

Take your time – the gentle heat will ensure a beautifully creamy sauce and will mean you won't end up with a mix that's altogether too firm.

Serves 4 (or 2 in our house)

tarragon chicken

Few children dislike roast chicken and, though it takes a while to cook, there's nothing complicated in the preparation. I often cook this when the children have friends round after school. It's absolutely scrumptious served with tons of roast potatoes.

1 chicken, organic, corn-fed
2 cloves of garlic
Small bunch of tarragon, chopped
Maldon salt
Butter

Chop the garlic into small pieces. Make some small incisions in the chicken breasts and thighs and push a small bit of garlic and tarragon under the skin.

Smear the chicken with butter and sprinkle the salt all over. Stand the chicken on a grill rack in the full-size roasting tin. Make a dome out of silver foil and put it over the chicken.

Slide the tin into the roasting oven on the lowest set of runners. Cook for 20 minutes per 500g (18 oz) plus 30 minutes.

Take the foil off about 45 minutes before the end of the cooking time to allow the chicken to brown.

Serve with mashed or roast potatoes, rice or a crisp green salad.

Serves 4

meatballs with spaghetti

When the children have overdosed on PlayStation or are becoming naughty, I often drag them into the kitchen to make this.

For the meatballs
250g (9 oz) of minced pork
250g (9 oz) of minced beef
1 egg
3 tablespoons of grated Parmesan
2 garlic cloves
1 tablespoon of chives, chopped
1 tablespoon of basil, chopped
4 tablespoons of breadcrumbs
Salt and black pepper
For the sauce
1 tablespoon of olive oil
1 onion, finely chopped
4 garlic cloves, chopped
Handful of basil, shredded
2 x 400g tins (14 fl oz) of organic tomatoes
150ml (5 fl oz) of water
Salt and freshly ground pepper
100ml (4 fl oz) of single cream

For the meatballs
Put all the ingredients into a bowl and mix with a wooden spoon. Once everything is combined, shape the mixture into balls.

For the sauce
Heat the olive oil in a large pan on the simmering plate. Add the onion and cook gently for about five minutes. Add the garlic and half the basil and cook for another couple of minutes. Add the tomatoes, the water and the seasoning. Cook for about 10 minutes. Add the cream, stir, then add the meatballs. Transfer to the simmering oven for about an hour, adding the remaining basil in the last few minutes. Serve the meatballs on top of large plates of steaming spaghetti.

Serves 6

Although this does take a little time to prepare,
it's well worth it – pure childhood comfort food.

comforting risotto

With an Aga, a risotto needs little attention as it spends most of its time in the simmering oven. It's impossibly comforting and, as many babies' first spoonful of food is rice, it's a taste most children adore.

Tablespoon of butter
2 chicken breasts, diced
1 onion, finely chopped
320g (11^1/$_2$ oz) of Arborio rice
1 glass of dry white wine (optional)
1 litre (1^3/$_4$ pints) of hot chicken or
   vegetable stock
^{1}/$_2$ tablespoon of butter
Freshly grated Parmesan

In a heavy bottomed oven-proof pan sauté the onion, chicken and bacon in the butter. Cook on the simmering plate for about 5 minutes.

Add the rice and mix well until it's coated and cook until it's utterly transparent. Add the wine if you want to and stir until it's evaporated or has been absorbed.

Move the pan to the boiling plate, add the stock and bring to the boil. Transfer it to the floor of the simmering oven and leave for around 20 minutes.

Check all the liquid has been absorbed and that the rice is tender and creamy, but still firm to the bite.

Stir in the butter and Parmesan and serve with salad.

Serves 4

best-ever chocolate cake

Moist, slightly gooey, with big chunks of chocolate, this is delicious served warm with ice cream. But it's also perfect for lunchboxes or after-school tea. Let the fun begin!

250g (8 oz) of softened butter
250g (8 oz) of golden caster sugar
4 eggs
Teaspoon of vanilla extract
3 tablespoons of Green & Black's cocoa powder
4 tablespoons of full-fat milk
250g (8 oz) of self-raising flour
100g (4$^1/_2$ oz) bar of best milk chocolate (I use Lindt)

Beat together the butter and sugar. Add the egg and vanilla extract. Mix in the cocoa powder and milk. Slowly add the flour, beating all the time to ensure the mixture doesn't get lumpy. Smash the chocolate to pieces (children adore doing this bit) or, alternatively, throw everything into an electric mixer and whiz for a few minutes.

Pour the cake mixture into a round greased tin. For a three- or four-oven Aga, place the cake tin on the grid shelf on the floor of the baking oven and cook for about 20–25 minutes.

For a two-oven Aga, place the cake tin on the grid shelf on the floor of the roasting oven and place the plain shelf on the second set of runners. Bake for about 20–25 minutes. Test with a knife or skewer.

Serves 4

Time to put on the aprons, hand out the wooden spoons and have some serious cooking fun!

spongy pear tart

My children adore this topsy-turvy recipe. It goes in one way and comes out the other. Much debate centres on the pattern the pears should make, but that's soon forgotten as it comes out of the Aga.

Tablespoon of butter
Tablespoon of golden syrup
Small tin of pears in syrup
125g (4 oz) of softened, unsalted butter
125g (4 oz) of caster sugar
2 eggs
125g (4 oz) of self-raising flour
Half a teaspoon of vanilla extract

Grease a small, round cake tin with the butter. Pour in the golden syrup and mix around a bit. Drain and slice the pears (keeping back a tablespoon of their syrup for later) and arrange at the bottom of the tin.

Beat together the butter and sugar. Add the egg, the vanilla extract and the pear syrup. Slowly add the flour, beating all the time to ensure the mixture doesn't get lumpy. Alternatively, you can throw everything into an electric mixer and whiz it for a few minutes.

Pour the cake mixture over the pears.

For a three- or four-oven Aga, place the cake tin on the grid shelf on the floor of the baking oven and cook for 20–25 minutes.

For a two-oven Aga, place cake tin on the grid shelf on the floor of the roasting oven and place the plain shelf on the second set of runners. Bake for about 20–25 minutes, then test with a knife or skewer. Serve warm with cream or ice cream.

Serves 6–8

fairy cakes

Every child should bake at least one batch of fairy cakes. The sheer joy of licking the cake mixture from the spoon or dying the icing a lurid shade is a quintessentially childish pleasure.

For the cakes
125g (4 oz) of softened unsalted butter
125g (4 oz) of caster sugar
Half a teaspoon of vanilla extract
2 eggs
125g (4 oz) of self-raising flour

The easiest way to make fairy cakes is to throw everything into a food processor, but much of the fun for children is in the mixing. So, with wooden spoon at the ready here's what to do...

Cream together the butter and sugar, add the vanilla extract and then the eggs. When the mixture has come together, start to add the flour a little at a time, beating until you've used it all. Spoon the mixture into paper cases lining a muffin tray.

For a three- or four-oven Aga, place the muffin tray on the grid shelf on the floor of the baking oven and cook for about 15–20 minutes.

For a two-oven Aga, place the muffin tray on the grid shelf on the floor of the roasting oven and place the plain shelf on the second set of runners. Bake for 10–12 minutes.

Makes about 12

See p113 for decorating tips.

No one should reach their teenage years without having made a batch of colourful fairy cakes...

decorating your fairy cakes

Here's where your child should be allowed to indulge in utter artistic freedom. A fairy cake decorated by oneself tastes infinitely nicer when you're small and parents should not try to dictate the pattern!

For the glacé icing
225g (8 oz) of icing sugar
2–4 tablespoons of hot water
Food colouring (optional)

Sift the icing sugar into a bowl. Slowly add enough water to give you a smooth icing that is thick enough to coat the back of a spoon. Add extra water if it is too thick or extra sugar if it becomes a little runny.

When it comes to food colouring, less is definitely more. If you don't want all the cakes to be iced in the same colour then remove a small amount of the icing to another bowl and add the smallest drip of colouring. You can always add more until you achieve the desired shade.

Some decorating tips
Plain white icing looks fab when topped by a single crystallised rose or violet petal.

Rice paper flowers are a nostalgia-trip for anyone who's reached 30 and are so pretty. Children can plonk one on a cake and feel they've created a work of art.

Dolly mixtures look and taste yummy and single colour dolly mixture fairy cakes have, to a five-year-old, an indefinable sophistication.

Writing icing now comes in handy little tubes, perfect for small hands, and in a wide array of colours. Older children can write messages, while smaller children can create their own patterns.

Tissue paper-lined boxes decorated by children and containing lovingly made cakes are fab gifts

mini pizzas

Making your own supper is such fun when you're small. Pizzas are perfect – they encourage a love of cooking while also allowing for boundless artistic enthusiasm. Get set for a mini adventure....

Pizza dough (see recipe on page 116)
400g (14 oz) tin of tomatoes
1 tablespoon of tomato purée
Olive oil
Salt and pepper
Two Mozzarella cheeses, sliced
Fresh basil leaves

Divide the dough into equal pieces. You can make any size pizzas you like. If you have too much dough, then bake some dough balls or garlic bread to go with your supper or some rolls for tomorrow's lunchboxes.

Set the pizza dough, evenly spaced, on greased baking sheets.

Open the tin of tomatoes and drain the juice. Blitz the tomatoes in a processor and add the purée, olive oil, salt and pepper. Blend gently. Spoon the tomato mixture over the pizza bases, distributing it evenly. Leave a gap around the edges so you'll get an uncovered crust.

Pop on the sliced Mozzarella and top with anything else you fancy – ham, mushrooms, sweetcorn, tuna, bacon, pepperoni, the list goes on.

Pop the baking sheet on to the floor of the roasting oven and bake for between 10 and 20 minutes, depending on the size of the pizza.

our daily bread

Freshly baked bread is heavenly and startlingly easy to make. I can't understand why any Aga owner would want a bread maker when the Aga is the ultimate bread making machine.

650g (1lb 7$^1/_2$ oz) of strong white bread flour
1 teaspoon of salt
$^1/_2$ teaspoon of sugar
1 sachet of instant dried yeast
Good splash of olive oil
400ml (14 fl oz) of warm water (1 part boiling, 2 parts cold)

Mix the dry ingredients together, add the olive oil and stir. Slowly start to add the water and mix until it becomes a dough.

Turn out on to a lightly floured surface and knead for about 10 minutes. You can use an electric mixer with a dough hook if you like, but there is something so wonderfully earthy about kneading it by hand that it would seem a shame. Put the dough back into the bowl and cover it with a clean tea towel. Then it needs to go somewhere warm. A surface next to the Aga is perfect. Leave for about an hour or until the dough has doubled in size.

Uncover and shape the dough into a loaf and put on a piece of Bake-O-Glide in a loaf tin or on a baking tray. Put it back in the warm place and leave for another 30 minutes. Then bake in the roasting oven, with the grid shelf on the floor, for about 20 minutes or until the bread is golden and sounds hollow when tapped.

Makes a standard white loaf

This dough makes a quite perfect pizza base.
Also, try dough balls with pasta dishes or salad

index

acknowledgements

Cooking is such a social activity, so it's brilliant to get as many people involved in the process as possible. Whether they're just hanging out in the kitchen, passing on hints and tips, loading the washing-up machine, or tasting and commenting, everyone is always welcome in my kitchen.

With this in mind, there are an awful lot of people to thank. So, here goes...

Firstly, thank you to everyone who contributed recipe ideas, ovens, cookware and advice. They include: Patty and Simon Page, Dawn Roads, Maggie, Pauline and Linda.

Thank you to Jon Croft, Meg Avent and Matt Inwood at Absolute Press, all of whom I adore.

Thank you also to Marry Berry and Lucy Young for being both inspirational and kind.

And, finally, thank you to my family – my husband, Tim, and my adorable children, Lucie, Tatti, Jack and Toby, who are constantly in the kitchen begging for more.